Introduction

The Open University
Walton Hall
Milton Keynes
MK7 6AA

First published 2010. Second edition 2011.

Edited and designed by The Open University.

Typeset by The Open University.

Printed by Bell & Bain Ltd, Glasgow.

978 1 8487 3915 4

2.1

Introduction

Chris Emlyn-Jones and Paula James

Contents

1   Introducing A330

1.1   Welcome

Welcome to A330. In the course of your study you are going to explore a topic which is integral to the whole of Greek and Roman culture: myth. It is literally true that you cannot study the Greeks and the Romans without encountering their myths in some form or other, and studying this aspect of the ancient world is often the best way of gaining an insight, in breadth and depth, into what their societies were really like. And because myth permeated all aspects of Greek and Roman life, in studying it you will be introduced to a broad range of original sources, both written and visual. Equally, these stories have had a profound influence on later cultures, right up to the present day (see Figure I), and you will also explore how classical myths have been received and interpreted during certain periods of history.

Figure I   Greek postage stamp, issued in 1983, with detail of a proto-Attic vase showing the blinding of the one-eyed monster Polyphemus by the hero Odysseus and his men, 670–660 BCE. Postal Museum, Hellenic Post, Athens. Photo: Hellenic Post, Athens. An illustration of the modern popular currency of Greek myth. The scene occurs in Homer's *Odyssey*, Book 9.

In writing A330 we are aware that you may be coming to it from a correspondingly wide variety of backgrounds – you may have studied other academic disciplines such as history, English, religious studies or philosophy. There is something here for all, and be reassured that we don't assume previous knowledge of the ancient world. From time to time you will be asked to look up background information on a particular topic, author, artist or historical period; and if you have absolutely no previous knowledge of the ancient world, there are suggestions for general background reading on the A330 website.

This Introduction comprises two weeks' work, culminating in a short assignment (TMA) in the third week, which is designed to orient you to A330 and to introduce the knowledge and skills you'll be needing (see the Assessment Booklet for further details). There are five sections to the Introduction:

1   Introducing A330 (a general description of A330 and its rationale)

2   Learning outcomes (what you will learn)

3   Structure, components and resources (including information on set books and the A330 website)

4   Resource orientation activities (a brief introduction to using your set reference books)

5   Icarus: entering the world of myth (leading to TMA 01)

Sections 1–4, which are primarily for information and familiarisation, will take approximately one week's study. Section 5, which involves work on several sources, will take one week by itself.

1.2   What is myth?

Activity

Take a minute or two to jot down how you think you would understand the term 'myth' if asked on the spot what it meant in normal conversation. (Don't take a long time – just some brief thoughts.)

Discussion

I wonder if, like me, you decided it was a word with rather ambivalent connotations. In conventional modern speech it tends to have a negative undertone, and is often used as a put-down in an argument: 'That's a complete myth!' (i.e. what you're saying is untrue). To describe a religious belief as a 'myth' is usually, in ordinary conversation, to express the view that it isn't true, or at least not literally so. At the same time, myths can often indicate powerful beliefs, which are widely held and influential, even if their truth-value is uncertain.

But 'myth' also has wider connotations outside this popular modern usage. The word is taken directly from the Greek word *muthos* (Greek 'u' is regularly rendered as 'y' in English, hence *myth*) which means 'story' or 'tale'. Although traditionally myths have often been divided up into a number of categories depending on type – such as folktales, legends or sagas – the essential ingredient of a myth is a story, told and retold in a variety of ways, to a variety of audiences and in a range of media – oral, written and in visual representation. Its being told and retold distinguishes it from an ordinary story, and indicates that it is important in some way to the societies which hear it.

As a broad category, therefore, myth throws up a number of different questions which may well reflect where you are coming from in your previous study.

- What is myth for and how does it arise?
- How does myth reflect or influence the dynamics of society, and how is it used and expressed by particular social groups?
- How are individual myths presented artistically in literature or painting?
- How do myths relate to religion or philosophy?
- What happens to myths when they are taken up by later cultures?

An attempt will be made to tackle all these questions in the course of A330. The list can in any case be very long, and simply reflects the power and ubiquity of myth.

In my discussion above about the ways myth is disseminated I hinted at the significance of oral transmission. For obvious reasons we have to concentrate on sources from literate societies, even if, occasionally, we get a glimpse of what lies behind them. It is probably true to say that all cultures have had and still have myths; perhaps, for all we know, going right back to the creators of Stone Age cave paintings. The vast majority of myths in most cultures have been disseminated orally from within societies without writing, and study of them tends to be the province of anthropologists and prehistorians. For us, however large our canvas, we are looking at very specific presentations of myth through sources which have been preserved over time and therefore happen to be accessible to us – the tip of an iceberg, so to speak.

1.3 What's so special about Greek and Roman myth?

It would be perfectly legitimate to study Icelandic, Germanic, Celtic or Indian myth, to name just a few cultures whose myths are rich, varied and comparatively well-known through literary and artistic media. However, if one is just choosing a single area, Greek and Roman myth has a great deal to recommend it. It has a particularly well-documented history gleaned from a rich variety of different sources which enable us to study it in a wide range of the kind of contexts I referred to above. It also has an important and very well-documented afterlife, sharing with Christianity the basis of medieval and Renaissance culture in Europe, as well as being influential in modern times. Moreover, when scholars in the nineteenth and twentieth centuries took up the theoretical study of myth as a phenomenon – what in general its function was and what it was based on – they turned predominantly to Greek and Roman myths, from the massive nineteenth-century study of Sir James Frazer's *The Golden Bough* (which you will meet in Block 1, Part 4), to the famous 'Oedipus complex' of the psychologist Sigmund Freud (itself derived from a Greek myth famously dramatised by the tragedian Sophocles in the fifth century BCE). In fact, a significant aspect of Greek and Roman myth is its reception in later cultural contexts – imaginative as well as theoretical – and you will have the opportunity to explore a fascinating example of this reception in Section 5 below, as well as later in your study (Block 3).

Note that it is myth in the Greek *and Roman* worlds which we are offering. In many books you may encounter references to '*Greek* myth', the assumption being that the Romans were simply adopting the Greek myths wholesale. It is true that many of the myths we will be studying originated in Greek culture and that the Romans often adopted and adapted the Greek stories rather than developing their own, so in a sense it is correct to call much of Roman myth derivative. But only in a very limited sense: not only did the Romans have myths of their own, as you will discover (Block 2), but, when they did adopt Greek myths, the Romans transformed them and used them in highly individual ways (see Figures II and III). And when later cultures viewed Greek myths, they did so through Roman eyes (at least until the eighteenth century CE). For example, the most influential figure in the afterlife of classical myth was the first-century CE poet Ovid, who will be the subject of a major study in Block 3. We are therefore aiming to balance exploration of the Greek and Roman worlds in roughly equal proportions.

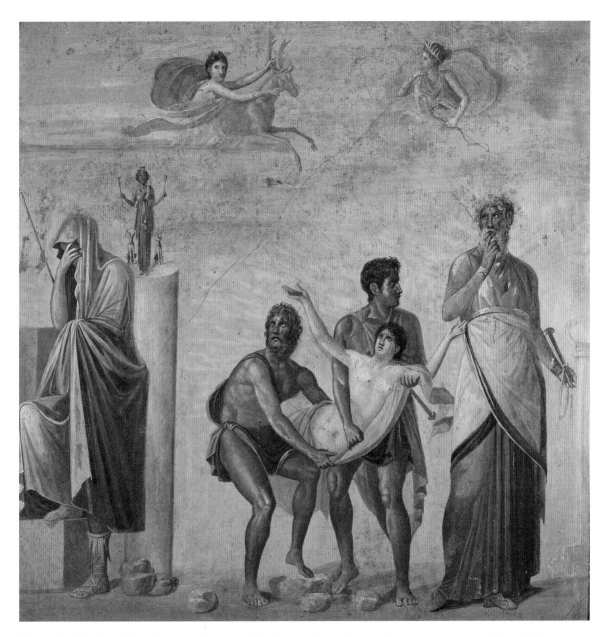

Figure II   Wall painting from the House of the Tragic Poet, Pompeii, showing the sacrifice of Iphigenia, first century CE, 126 × 123 cm. Museo Archeologico Nazionale, Naples. Photo: akg-images/Erich Lessing. A Roman depiction of an important scene from Greek legend: the leader of the Greeks, Agamemnon, sacrifices his daughter to enable the Greek army to sail to Troy.

Figure III   Wall painting from the House of Jason, Pompeii, showing Europa carried off by Zeus in one of his many disguises (a bull), before 79 CE. Museo Archeologico Nazionale, Naples. Photo: akg-images/Nimatallah. Another Roman representation of a Greek legend.

1.4   The main focus of A330

Before we started devising A330, some preliminary decisions had to be made with regard to direction and focus, knowledge of which will help you to understand why the structure is as it is. Two main aspects had to be tackled.

- Greek and Roman myths, as I mentioned at the beginning, permeate more or less every aspect of society and culture, and the range and ramifications of the subject are virtually endless (a glance at the nearly 800 pages of your main set reference book, *Classical Mythology* by Mark P.O. Morford and Robert J. Lenardon, will give you some idea of the size of the subject). So we have had to make choices. In the four main blocks of A330 we have chosen to focus on certain key aspects of the subject, chosen first for intrinsic importance and interest, and secondly to cover a representative range of topics and sources. Actually, the range of the subject is entirely appropriate for study at OU level 3: in the later stages of A330 there will be ample opportunity for you to work outwards from the topics chosen to pursue particular interests of your own, and there will be help in doing so.

- Greek and Roman myth as an area of study could equally well be called 'Greek and Roman' or 'classical' *mythology* (see the title used by Morford and Lenardon). We had considerable discussion and debate about this; our finally chosen title reflects a desire to keep focused in the first instance on specific contexts – artistic, cultural and historical – and work outwards from these. But no study of classical myth can ignore entirely the considerable body of theory surrounding the myths – what they are for, what they represent, how they function and how they relate to other modes of thinking. Rather than introduce theory as a separate study, however, we shall be looking at specific theoretical approaches as and when their introduction is appropriate.

1.5   Reading for those new to classical antiquity

During your study we will not spend a lot of time filling in historical background, although we will supply plentiful pointers and advice, where necessary, on where to look. And if you are coming to the ancient world for the first time, perhaps from study of some other subject, you are strongly advised to do some preliminary reading to orient yourself and become familiar with the broad outlines of the cultural area you will be studying. Again, suggestions can be found on the A330 website.

2 Learning outcomes

In the course of studying A330 you can expect to:

1 Gain in-depth knowledge of a specific range of myths and mythical characters.

2 Consider how certain myths function in a range of contexts – historical, social and cultural.

3 Study and analyse the presentation of myths in a variety of sources – such as poetry, drama, history, philosophy, art, architecture and archaeology – evaluating the context of the evidence and how different contexts may relate to each other.

4 Develop the ability to write a well thought-out analysis of texts and artistic representations and produce essays containing logical argument and analysis at an appropriate level.

5 Become familiar with critical analysis of the reception of Greek and Roman myth, including a range of theoretical approaches and modern scholarship relating to classical mythology.

6 Develop a degree of independence in learning to the extent that you are able to do your own analyses, using the skills you have learned in the course of study, including research via the internet and libraries.

These are the envisaged outcomes of A330, formally set out. But there are three key points contained in them you need especially to note at this stage:

- The emphasis is not on covering *everything* but to focus in critical depth on *specifics* (myths/issues), and follow them through a variety of sources/contexts/critical questions.

- A330 has been conceived with an upward learning curve, as appropriate for third-level (honours) study; it has been designed to take you from second level at the beginning, to a level appropriate to the completion of an honours degree at the end. Accordingly towards the end of A330 you should expect to be able to work with a degree of independence (see outcome 6 above).

- There is no examination, but a final examinable component, which counts for 50 per cent of the total marks (see Assessment Booklet).

3 Structure, components and resources

3.1 Structure

As stated above (Section 1.3), the focus of A330 is roughly equally divided between the Greek and Roman worlds. The core consists of four main teaching blocks, each focusing on a particular aspect of the subject. These will be supported by the reading and studying of a variety of source material (primary and secondary sources and reference information) and DVD-ROM activities. The main blocks are titled as follows:

Block 1   The myth of Hippolytus and Phaedra

Block 2   Rome: myth and history

Block 3   Ovid and the reception of myth

Block 4   Myth and reason in classical Greece

The rationale of this structure will, I hope, become clear as you study. One glance will tell you that the order of the blocks is not historical, from A (early Greece) to Z (late Rome). Rather it is basically driven by what we see as a number of different perspectives on the central issue of myth as a phenomenon in the cultural life of Greece and Rome and its later influence, while at the same time exploring the wide range of sources through which myth was expressed. With a large and somewhat amorphous subject it's always a good idea to start with specifics, so Block 1 explores the development of a single myth relating to specific individuals (Hippolytus and Phaedra) from the Greek to the Roman and on into the early Christian period. Block 2 considers the way Roman myths were influential in specific social and historical contexts. Block 3 concentrates on arguably the most important literary figure in the expression and transformation of myth, the Latin poet Ovid, and his later influence. Block 4 returns to Greece, looking at the earliest developments of philosophy, science and medicine in relation to myth, and raises general questions about this relationship.

Assessment

You will be expected to submit five tutor-marked assignments (TMAs) and a final examinable component. Full details of the assessment policy and the specific questions for each TMA (with cut-off dates) can be found in the Assessment Booklet. Your online study planner (on the A330 website) also provides an overview of your schedule of study and a reminder of the cut-off dates for your assignments.

3.2 Components

- Four written and illustrated teaching blocks (plus this Introduction)
- Set books:

    Euripides, *Hippolytus*, in Davie, J. (trans.) (2003) *Medea and Other Plays*, rev. edn, London, Penguin

    Ovid, *Metamorphoses*, in Raeburn, D. (trans.) (2004) *Metamorphoses*, London, Penguin

    Morford, M.P.O. and Lenardon, R.J. (2009) *Classical Mythology* (international 8th edn), New York and Oxford, Oxford University Press (abbreviated to M&L)

    Grimal, P. (2005) *The Penguin Dictionary of Classical Mythology* (trans. A. Maxwell-Hyslop; ed. S. Kershaw), London, Penguin (abbreviated to Penguin Dictionary)

- Textual Sources 1 and 2 (written primary and secondary sources relating to the four blocks)
- Visual Sources (visual primary and secondary sources relating to the four blocks)
- DVD-ROM (audio-visual and interactive material)
- Assessment Booklet (information on TMAs and the ECA)
- A330 website (online resources)

3.3 Resources

In order to find your way through the different types of resource provided, the best course of action is to use the teaching blocks as your basic guide, or the 'bridge of the ship'. From these you will be directed out to other materials at suitable points.

It may, however, be useful at this point just to make some clear distinctions between the function of different materials. I'd like to isolate three main types of materials.

1   *Primary sources* are scattered around the different components (necessarily so, because they come in different media and forms). There are two complete texts – Euripides' *Hippolytus* and Ovid's

Metamorphoses – which you will need to read in their entirety (or, in the case of Ovid, in substantial chunks). Other shorter extracts from ancient sources are available in both volumes of the Textual Sources. Visual sources are to be found not only in the Visual Sources book, but also on the DVD-ROM and the A330 website. This is essentially the 'raw material' on which we base our work.

2   *Secondary sources* are also found in the Textual Sources books, but they fulfil a completely different function from the primary sources: they comprise articles, book chapters and so on, written by scholars as a result of studying the primary sources. This gives us ideas, theories, opinion and analysis, which we need to assess. Modern scholarship is also to be found on the DVD-ROM, which presents visual evidence and audio interviews with contemporary experts, looking at and commenting on the ancient evidence. You will also encounter in the blocks references to other books or articles referred to as 'Optional reading'. This often involves having access to specialist libraries (although an increasing amount of this material is available online, and, where it is, you will be told). Don't let reference to this material generate anxiety if you find that access to it is difficult or impossible: it is entirely optional as the name suggests, and not necessary for the completion of TMAs. It is there for interest, and possibly to be picked up later, if relevant to any work you may decide to do on your examinable component.

3   *Reference works*, clearly, contain a lot of information or background and are not intended to be read through from start to finish, but to be consulted as and when. On a factual level, M&L probably contains almost everything you are ever likely to want to know about Greek and Roman mythology (and much that you won't: I defy you to read it through from cover to cover). It also contains a wealth of primary texts, illustrations and figures; very useful indexes; and encapsulated boxes giving information on certain authors and topics (see Section 4 below). For quick and handy reference, there is also the Penguin Dictionary, as a supplement to M&L.

Further important sources of reference are online resources, accessible via the A330 website: specialist encyclopedias and dictionaries, not forgetting Wikipedia. You should find these extremely useful, and they will also give you an opportunity to do some searching of your own. Block 1 starts by directing you to an orientation exercise which includes guidelines on the use of some of these resources.

In order to help you find your way around ancient Greece and Rome, there are a number of maps available in your resources. The frontispiece to M&L shows a map of Greece, Crete and the Aegean Sea, which we have printed in a larger, colour format as Plate I in Visual Sources. M&L also contains a map of Roman Italy (p. 656) and Rome itself (p. 672), and you will be engaging with an interactive map of ancient Rome on the DVD-ROM later on.

4 Resource orientation activities

4.1 Morford and Lenardon (M&L)

Activity

M&L contains some very useful and comprehensive indexes, as mentioned above. Look up the following as I describe them (pp. 781ff.).

- *Glossary of mythological words and phrases in English* (pp. 781–94). Classical mythology has a number of terms/names/phrases which won't be immediately obvious; you probably won't need half of these, but if you do come across a word or phrase you don't understand and it is not explained, this glossary is almost bound to have it.

- *The Greek spelling of names* (pp. 795–8). You will come across different ways of spelling certain names; this is because the Romans, when incorporating Greek names into Latin, adapted them to their language. These differences are not very great, for example: Achilleus/Achilles, Herakles/Hercules, Hippolytos/Hippolytus. If you have encountered classical mythology before you are probably more familiar with the Latin form, which we use here. However, I cannot emphasise strongly enough that this is not a major issue; either form will be perfectly acceptable in your written work. Note that there are a few cases where the Romans adopted Greek mythological figures and gave them a different name; these are very few, and tend to be major figures, for example: Zeus/Jupiter, Hera/Juno, Athene/Minerva, Poseidon/Neptune, Artemis/Diana and Aphrodite/Venus. (We won't always state an alternative Greek or Roman name for mythological figures but you can look them up in M&L or the Penguin Dictionary if you need to.)

- *Index of authors, artists, composers and titles* (I-1–I-11). These are the sources used by M&L. Self-explanatory, except to note that this index covers not only ancient but also modern authors.

- *Index of mythological and historical persons, places and subjects* (I-12–I-43). This is probably the most useful index in M&L. It contains a comprehensive list of all the people and places you are likely to meet, with page references to the main text. Note that references to illustrations/figures are in bold type.

If you simply want swift basic information, then you might prefer to use the Penguin Dictionary, the use of which is straightforward and self-explanatory. Both M&L and the Penguin Dictionary are essential in their different ways; when you are not specifically directed to one or the other, experience should decide which of these you will want personally to consult in any given instance.

Activity

Read M&L, pp. 25–9, 'Appendix to Chapter 1: Sources for classical mythology' (a useful summary). Note the general types of sources found, and anything which strikes you as unusual.

Discussion

I appreciate that the second part of my direction was rather open-ended, but what you may have noticed as odd (especially if you haven't had any previous acquaintance with the subject) is that all the earliest sources for Greek mythology are poetry and drama. The epic poet Homer starts it all off in the eighth century BCE with his *Iliad* and *Odyssey*, and in the fifth century BCE, we have important dramatic representations of myths (one of which you will be studying in detail in Block 1). Only in the fifth century BCE, known conventionally as the 'Classical period' of Greece, do we begin to see prose accounts, for example in the work of the historian Herodotus. But in none of this do we find works which actually catalogue and discuss myth for its own sake; this comes later with what are called 'mythographers'. This tells us something about how the Greeks (and later the Romans) viewed myth. They were not in the first instance concerned to catalogue it; it was on the whole not something to be analysed objectively, but part of their living experience and their past, whether looked at poetically, through the eyes of Homer or Hesiod, or historically, with Herodotus.

Another point I thought strange was that by 'sources' here M&L evidently understand just 'written sources'; they don't, at this stage, talk about the visual evidence. Clearly this has not stopped them introducing very many excellent visual images of mythology in the text. But note that in A330 when we talk about 'sources' we consider equally written and visual material, and you will be working extensively on both.

Activity

Now take a look at some of the ancient sources quoted in Chapter 3 of M&L (they are distinguished by grey bars in the left-hand margin). What impression do you get of the literary style of these sources?

Discussion

I hope you weren't put off by the prose layout – these sources are actually in verse form, as, I think, the high-flown language makes clear. If you've read a few of these extracts from Chapter 3, you'll also have got some idea of the content. Everything is personalised: what we have here are roughly accounts of the origins of the world, but not as we would view it. The Greeks at this point saw things through the actions of gods and goddesses, though sometimes looking like natural phenomena in thin disguise – what we call 'theogony' rather than 'cosmogony'. These terms, and the concept of 'creation myths' in general, will be discussed further in Block 4.

To round off, I'd like to make two further points about the way M&L organise the material.

1   Their chapters are 'topic-based'. They are concerned to give their reader all the information available on a particular topic in the same place; so, on occasion, sources are assembled from different periods (especially the visual sources) without much discussion of the historical gaps between them. This can be very useful, but you need to be aware of this underlying organisational principle in the book. In A330 you will need to gain understanding of the way certain myths developed historically, and in the case of the major sources, you will need to get a reasonably good idea of who lived when and so on.

2   The illustrations in M&L are very useful, especially with their full captions and (although, as we saw above, the authors don't call them 'sources') they emphasise the fact that visual records are as important, in their way, for telling and interpreting the stories as the written sources. They are also particularly helpful in showing how later artists interpret the mythological material.

4.2   Mythological characters

In your initial encounter with the subject of classical myth, the plethora of names can be bewildering. There is, however, a definite hierarchy of importance (and a large percentage of the names you come across are not very important). Greek and Roman mythology is populated by, very roughly, three categories of figures:

- fully immortal gods (e.g. the god Zeus)
- a rather amorphous category of semi-divine beings (e.g. the hero Heracles, who enjoyed at different times mortal and immortal status, nymphs)
- mortals (e.g. heroes like Achilles, Odysseus)

A good way of getting a grip on all this is to look at the main characteristics of a handful of the most important gods. These are:

Zeus, Hera (see Figure IV), Apollo, Athena, Poseidon, Hephaestus, Aphrodite, Ares, Hermes, Demeter and Artemis. This is the 'first team', some of whom will tend to crop up frequently. They are called Olympian gods because most of them lived with Zeus, the chief of the gods and the most powerful, on Mount Olympus (a mythical place – although there is geographically, of course, a high mountain called Olympus in northern Greece). They tend to have 'provinces' of influence: for example, Poseidon has lordship of the sea, while the province of Aphrodite is (as you probably already know) love. Zeus, the general overlord, has mighty power, illustrated, among other things, by his thunderbolt (see Figure V).

Activity

Find out more about the characteristics of these Olympian gods.

Note that M&L may actually be a bit confusing here for a first read, since they insist on telling you everything about the characteristics of the gods and their families as they go (and please do ignore, for the present, the 'family trees', which feature a lot of names you will never hear of again). Using the 'Index of mythological and historical persons, places and subjects' will help.

An alternative plan would be to look up each of these mythological figures in the Penguin Dictionary. Here, arranged alphabetically, you will find short helpful paragraphs on all of the mythological figures you are investigating.

Or you can look online at, for example, the *Oxford Classical Dictionary* (accessible via the A330 website). (Incidentally, don't worry if you are uncertain about locating online materials: there will be a directed exercise at the beginning of Block 1.)

How far you go with this activity is up to you, depending on how much time you have left in this week's work. You may want to go systematically through my list, or, alternatively, to browse. I'll leave this one open-ended.

Figure IV   Limestone metope from Temple E ('Temple of Hera'), Selinunte, Sicily, showing Zeus and Hera, *c*.460 BCE, height 162 cm. Museo Archeologico Nazionale, Palermo, Italy. Photo: akg-images/ Erich Lessing. This relief sculpture represents the marriage of the chief of the gods, Zeus, to his bride, the goddess Hera.

Figure V   Bronze statuette of Zeus with a thunderbolt, *c.*470 BCE, found at Dodona, north-west Greece, height 13.5 cm. Staatliche Museen, Berlin, Antikensammlung, misc. 10561. Photo: bpk/Antikensammlung, SMB/Christa Begall. Zeus is shown here in dynamic pose with his most characteristic weapon.

4.3   Introduction to the DVD-ROM

To finish off this first part of the Introduction, and before you go on to Section 5, take a look now at the introductory section of the DVD-ROM.

5 Icarus: entering the world of myth

5.1 Introduction

Over the next week you will be working on one short mythic narrative, the death of Icarus. This 'taster' of a myth from Ovid's *Metamorphoses* (one of your set books) will acclimatise you to reading and responding to a mythical story with an extremely varied afterlife. As you delve deeper into the impact and implications of the Icarus story you should keep in mind the range of approaches to, and indeed definitions of, myth that have already been suggested in the first four sections of this Introduction. Ovid's approach to myth as literary narrative is sophisticated and self-conscious, adding complex dimensions to the process and function of myth-making in ancient culture.

One aim in studying Icarus first of all is to help you contextualise the myth of Hippolytus and Phaedra, which will be the theme of Block 1. Without becoming too involved at this stage with the intricacies and intimacies of this dysfunctional royal family on the island of Crete, you can at least locate Icarus' and Daedalus' story within the larger framework of tragic events surrounding Minos, the Cretan king, and Theseus, the Athenian prince.

This week's work is also intended to prepare you for your study of Ovid in Block 3, where you will be assessing his work more thoroughly in its historical context. Many mythical stories familiar to a modern readership have been filtered through an Ovidian lens, and for this reason we have decided on an early introduction to the poet. Very few Graeco-Roman mythic narratives escaped his attention even if some crop up in unexpected places and only feature by brief allusion.

In Block 3 you will also learn in more depth about what is loosely called 'reception studies' and Ovid's importance for this academic field. A myth that has received the Ovidian treatment frequently acquires layers that need stripping back in order to rediscover the original core. Seeing Ovid as a 'receiver' requires the researcher to backtrack through Ovid's own sources and identify how the poet accessed and redeployed the literary and artistic material at his disposal. My metaphor of the Ovidian lens above suggests that filtering as well as layering is part of the poet's technique. However, the main focus of reception studies is the way in which the ancient text or motifs have been 'received' by subsequent cultures and reworked by their artists and writers.

Sampling Ovid in this week's work will involve the exciting activity of probing deeper into his influence on both the matter and the method of myth-telling in the literary and visual arts for centuries after his death. The presence of mythical themes, figures and motifs in popular culture is attracting an increasing amount of scholarly attention in the twenty-first century. Ovid's legacy is likely to loom large in the study of myths in the modern media, just as it has in scholarly works on mythical strands and subject matter from the medieval and Renaissance periods up to the twentieth century.

5.2   Ovid as mythographer and myth-maker

Publius Ovidius Naso, to give Ovid his three full names as a Roman citizen, was born in Sulmo (modern Sulmona), Italy in 43 BCE and died in exile at Tomis on the Black Sea coast (modern Constanţa, Romania) in 17 or 18 CE. You will be given more detailed background on Ovid in Block 3 but for present purposes you might like to start by regarding him as a mythographer or myth collector. The reason for this is his epic poem *Metamorphoses*, written at Rome and in Latin around the end of the first century BCE, which has proved to be a treasure house of Greek and Roman myths throughout the centuries. You will be finding out more about Ovid's organising principles and literary legacies in his epic poem later in Block 3.

Metamorphoses continues to function as a 'myth-kitty' – a notion coined and dismissed by the poet Philip Larkin (1982, p. 69) – but Ovid was not producing this *magnum opus* to be a mere catalogue for future cultures. There are some parallels between Ovid and the nineteenth-century scholar Sir James Frazer (who will figure at the end of Block 1) as both authors made connections between themes and characters across different myths. The kind of thematic superstructures Ovid and Frazer created – in their very different ways – have proved enormously influential on ideas about the meaning of myth and its function in society.

As I indicated above, Ovid was a receiver and also a refashioner (in his own day) of mythical material. He adapted and combined well-known narratives in ingenious ways but also brought to the fore less familiar, small-scale stories from Greek and Roman legend and put these on the mythic map for future generations. His use of an epic frame for such disparate and narratively fluid material was in itself challenging and innovative. In his prologue to *Metamorphoses* (1.1–4) Ovid claims to weave together stories of transformation in a 'continuous' song.

5.3   Icarus as symbol and signifier

The myth of Daedalus and Icarus, the father and son who escaped from the island of Crete on wings, is told in Book 8 of Ovid's *Metamorphoses*. Icarus has become the more familiar of the two characters as the ancient high-flyer who fell from the sky when the wax that secured his wings was melted by the sun.

Activity

Read M&L, pp. 598–607. You'll find that M&L use extracts from Ovid's narrative which you will later read in full in your set book, the Penguin translation (Ovid is clearly a key source in any compilation of myths).

Locate the Daedalus and Icarus story within the larger mythic narratives of Theseus and Minos and pinpoint the main sequence of events.

As noted in Section 4 above, M&L do have a tendency to go into overdrive on the detail and the genealogies, introducing marginal characters and subplots. This is comprehensive but can become confusing at times, so don't be discouraged.

Discussion

Icarus' story connects up with a number of narrative passageways centred on the island of Crete (where Daedalus, the legendary artificer and craftsman, constructed a maze, the Labyrinth, to conceal and control the Minotaur). Daedalus was himself effectively imprisoned on the island (the king barred his exit by sea) and so was unable to return with his son, Icarus, to Athens or find sanctuary away from the harsh regime at Crete.

You may have already known about other mythic strands associated with the Labyrinth (which I alluded to in my introduction to this section). The Athenian hero, Theseus, slayed the Minotaur, the half-man, half-bull offspring of queen Pasiphaë, with the help of Ariadne, daughter of King Minos. The Cretan princess Phaedra, who later married Theseus (even though he had abandoned her sister, Ariadne, his guide through the Labyrinth), developed a destructive and tragic passion for her stepson Hippolytus. These strange sexual couplings (or attempts at them – Phaedra is scorned and takes her revenge) stem from a curse on the descendants of the sun god, Helios. Aphrodite punished Helios for his exposure of her affair with Ares by decreeing that the female descendants of the sun would select and pursue inappropriate and disastrous partners. Phaedra and Hippolytus and their mythic trajectory are of course the focus of Block 1.

Activity

Think about any medium (from art, literature, film, television, or even perhaps a scientific article) in which you may have encountered Icarus. It might be the briefest of allusions or simply the use of his name to conjure up the miracle of 'man' or a man in flight. In what way is his myth used?

M&L have a good example of Icarus as an image for the aviator (the print by Matisse on p. 606). Plates II and III in the Visual Sources book give you two more examples: Saraceni's and Rubens' paintings of Icarus. (Clearly both canonical and contemporary artists have been intrigued by Icarus' tragic fate.) You could also look up 'Icarus' on the internet.

Discussion

As both character and image, Icarus continues to turn up in unexpected places, from scientific papers to use in advertising. Icarus has become a symbol for heroic daring (the crew of space shuttles that did not survive) but his flying and falling have been given a psychological timbre as well as a physical expression in all kinds of literature from poems to thrillers. Before I did any organised investigation of the range of Icarus-related texts I jotted down a few resonances of the myth from memory (including the two famous texts I shall be asking you shortly to engage with during your week's study).

For instance, some years ago, I read a rather unpleasant whodunit (verging on horror) entitled *Icarus* (by Russell Andrews) where living in skyscrapers and working at the top invite envy and murder. Recently (January 2009) I listened to a play on Radio 4 by Jonathan Davidson entitled *Icarus Falling*. The protagonist is an artist who, though successful, is having a disconcerting time with his paintings as they have started 'talking back' to him. He takes up gliding and flying in Cornwall (to the dismay of his wife and dealer) but this enables him to see the world from a whole new perspective. Davidson has accessed the myth for more than one metaphorical purpose.

Then there was a deodorant commercial from the 1990s which featured a shapely young woman with wings who successfully flew across a strait of water and landed safely on the other side of the ravine. The voice-over simply said: 'Icarus had a sister!' As the success of her flight was due to being sweet-smelling this was not exactly a feminist tract (empowerment comes from being a consumer of the right kind of scent) but it was an intriguing use of the myth nevertheless.

A Google internet search yielded a fascinating but random range of Icarus-related themes with plenty of examples from popular culture and, inevitably, marketing (e.g. lights and lampshades with the brand name 'Icarus'). Popular contemporary music boasted a long list of Icarus references, from Joni Mitchell's lyrics about airwoman Amelia Earhart ('Amelia', 1976), to Queen's song, 'No One But You (Only the Good Die Young)' (1997). In 2003, the band Thrice focused on Daedalus' perspective on the tragedy with a track entitled 'The Melting Point of Wax'. In popular song Icarus regularly represents the alienation of the artist and the consequences of breaking out of boundaries, both cultural and social.

Refining the search to 'the myth of Icarus in art and literature' produced various reference books and sites and took me back to Ovid (where all mythological roads tend to lead). In order to collect examples from a more stable source than the internet, I consulted Jenny March's entry on Icarus in the *Cassell Dictionary of Classical Mythology* (1998, p. 212). (This book is out of print but still available and it has the great advantage of citing classical references.) March offered just two literary legacies of the myth, one being the Icarus allusion in W.B. Yeats' poem, 'An Irish Airman Foresees his Death'.

March also quotes an eighteenth-century author, Philippe Destouches: 'Le ciel fut son désir, la mer son sépulture/est-il plus beau dessein ou plus riche tombeau?' (The sky was his desire, the sea his sepulchre/is there a more beautiful aim or a richer tomb?). However, I discovered that this stanza is also ascribed to the poet Philippe Desportes (1546–1605) and *sépulture* is sometimes a feminine noun (*sa sépulture*). I thought this was quite a salutary lesson in the occasional slippery nature of literary sources, even those that are not ancient and fragmentary.

My last port of call was volume 1 of the *Oxford Guide to Classical Mythology in the Arts, 1300–1990s* (1993, pp. 587–93) which gives a wide range of paintings, poems, ballets and operas devoted to the myth of Icarus, demonstrating the popularity of the story through the ages and across genres.

5.4   Daedalus and Icarus in *Metamorphoses*

Activity

Read Ovid's story of Icarus (*Metamorphoses* 8.182–235).

- How does Ovid portray the characters of Daedalus and Icarus?
- How might Ovid be manipulating our emotions?

Discussion

The following comments are not, of course, off the top of my head, as I have studied the myth and Ovid in detail over a number of years; but I think, as a reader who has perhaps been asked for the first time to make a critical response to the myth, you may well have reacted to Ovid's narrative in a similar way.

Almost immediately in the text Daedalus speaks for himself, outlining his dilemma succinctly and appraising the reader of his action plan. I thought that this invited us as readers into Daedalus' mind and set up a sympathetic resonance, as well as making the manufacture of the wings a tense dramatic moment. Ovid renders Daedalus' dilemma all the more poignant because he is trying to escape with his young son, Icarus. Devising drastic measures to escape, Daedalus knows he is taking a huge risk in attempting flight. He invests all his legendary skills as a craftsman in the design of wings for himself and Icarus.

Icarus is depicted as a boy rather than an adolescent; he gets in his father's way in the workshop and has no real inkling of the danger he is about to face. Lines 195–200 depict a meddling child, a familiar scene with tragic resonances: Ovid's readers (who would not need reminding about the myth) knew that the successful completion of the wings would mean the fall and death of Icarus. The heedlessness of the boy is a fatal characteristic; he will ignore his father's advice and soar towards the sun.

Before Icarus plummets to his death with his horrified father wailing his name, 'no longer a father' (line 231) (Ovid twists the emotional knife deeper here), he and Daedalus have enjoyed a brief but god-like view of the world. Angler, shepherd and ploughman have gazed up in wonder at them, but the glory is short-lived. The name 'Icarus' appears three times (lines 231–2), uttered by the desperate father as he looks down for his lost son.

David Raeburn's translation captures this threefold lament, but not all translators follow the Latin so closely. A.D. Melville, for instance, renders the two lines as: 'His wretched father, now no father, cried/"Oh, Icarus, where are you? Icarus/Where shall I look, where find you?"'

(1986, p. 178). However, he does repeat 'where' three times, so has intentionally retained the emphasis and rhythm of the repetition. In this way Melville keeps the literary artifice intact, but a cultural context has been lost because the repetition of the name in Raeburn's translation evokes features of a formal lament. The custom at Roman funerals was to call upon the corpse thrice by name (possibly to 'waken' the dead, in case they were actually in a catatonic trance) so the passing over of Icarus is ritually marked by Ovid before the burial even takes place.

Activity

Now read about Daedalus and Perdix (*Metamorphoses* 8.236–59).

- Does this alter our perspective on Daedalus, the grieving father?
- Can you suggest why Ovid delays the information about Perdix?

Discussion

The partridge is Perdix, Daedalus' apprentice. Ovid's educated readership would probably be familiar with the background story but the modern reader may be finding out for the first time that Daedalus was fleeing justice and retribution when he left Athens and took refuge in Crete. Daedalus had tried to murder his nephew, Talos, who had been entrusted to him as a second son to learn the craftsman's trade, but whose remarkable talents inspired jealous rage in his teacher. The goddess Minerva (Greek name, Athena) changed Talos into the partridge (Latin *perdix*) so he was saved from a fatal fall.

Talos (sometimes called Calos) becomes Perdix and this provides the actual transformation that justifies the presence of Icarus' story in a text about changes in form; and yet it could be argued that Daedalus and Icarus are imitating birds if not actually physically metamorphosing into something else. The murdered nephew is transformed into the partridge, a bird that has paradoxically (but logically given the manner of the boy's death) a horror of heights and nests close to the ground. The partridge rejoices at Icarus' death and Daedalus' grief.

Ovid has used a telling phrase as Icarus and Daedalus embark upon their flight. In line 214 Daedalus commands his son to follow 'as he taught him the skills that would prove his downfall'. A.D. Melville renders this as 'the father schooling Icarus in a fateful apprenticeship' (1986, p. 177). Daedalus has coached his son in the art of flight but this condemns the lad to death. There could also be a hint here of Perdix's fate, who, when entrusted to Daedalus' protection, succeeded in his work at his peril. He, too, was a victim of the overambitious craftsman.

Ovid closes the Daedalus narrative with an aetiological myth, explaining why the partridge behaves as it does – possibly Perdix is supposed to be the 'first' partridge. (*Aetia* is the Greek for 'cause', so aetiological myths often explain the origin of a species or something about their attributes.) Does Ovid mean to alter our perspective and undercut the sympathy we feel for Daedalus by this flashback technique?

There are times when even the ancient reader might feel led along by Ovid, even though they were in touch with the 'surround' stories of many major myths and would have this information already. In other words, Ovid's readership would be aware of Daedalus' crime against Perdix and Daedalus' designing of a labyrinth where, every fourteen years, Athenian boys and girls were slaughtered by the Minotaur.

Ovid is a master of allusion, cross-referencing, reprising and prefiguring not just within the confines of his epic but also shifting the spotlight on to hitherto marginalised figures in the myths. Icarus' fall is a brief episode, and although he was represented in ancient art, the literature of Greece and Rome tended to focus on the character of Daedalus whose remarkable talent formed the fulcrum of several key myths. Ovid's reconstruction of the boy's last moments are so vivid that Icarus became foregrounded, representing a tragic loss not just of life, but of human endeavour and artistic aspiration.

Overall, I would say that in *Metamorphoses* Ovid perfected the art of theorising myths as he narrated them, suggesting a psychological subtext here, an artistic symbol there, a metaphor on power at one moment, and a crisis of human identity the next. So, the adult reader is unlikely to 'just read' Ovid for the stories but will rapidly become engrossed in interpreting their motifs, themes and mixed messages. I am not suggesting that Ovid is producing a theory or theories of myth but he is clearly manipulating myths to yield their full potential as cultural, social and ideological barometers. In fact, Ovid encapsulates many of the characteristics of myth you will find throughout A330.

5.5 Bruegel and Auden

I would like you now to explore how far Ovid's own agenda (artistic, personal and, to some extent, ideological) has shaped two famous representations of Icarus in painting (Bruegel's *Landscape with the Fall of Icarus*) and poetry (W.H. Auden's 'Musée des Beaux Arts'). These subsequent versions of the myth may on the surface depart from Ovid's narrative, and the poem I have selected is actually reacting to the painting in the first instance, and is, therefore, 'once removed' from Ovid.

If you have acquired some skills of visual analysis or feel comfortable with literary critiques of twentieth-century poetry, then both the painting and the poem will, I hope, prompt you to ask questions about their form and composition. If not, then you can follow the guidelines below; these will help you to analyse artistic and literary techniques in the retelling of the myth. In these separate boxes I have provided a brief biography of Bruegel and Auden plus a few central characteristics (or 'tools of the trade') of their chosen genres which can be fruitfully applied to their texts.

Bruegel and his work

Pieter Bruegel the Elder was born around 1520 and died in 1569. He was master of the Antwerp Guild in 1552 and is renowned for his landscape painting (the Alps and Italian scenery inspired his work). But his subsequent reputation fluctuated with positive and negative reactions to a satiric and graphic style of representation: pictures of peasants, life in the raw, allusions to contemporary troubles and so on – he lived and worked in turbulent times with constant political and religious turmoil in the Netherlands.

What to look for in the painting

Well, the subject matter is an obvious starting point and the title tells the viewer quite a lot. Although a variety of activities may be taking place, the way the figures and objects relate to each other (foreground, background, at the margins of the frame) reveal something of the painter's priorities.

Size matters: if you are not viewing the original in an art gallery, you should at least work out the proportions of a picture and its impact (ranging from intimate cameo to larger-than-life and all the gradations in between). This leads into the area of *perspective* and how the spectator's viewpoint is manipulated – how distant or how close the objects might be and whether we are outside or inside the space the painting occupies.

Is there a focal point that draws us in? Is there an aerial or atmospheric perspective? (Optical effects can be achieved with the creation of dust particles to mute far away objects.) Is there an obvious vanishing point – do apparently parallel lines converge towards a single point on the horizon?

How are colour and tone deployed? Are the colours warm, bright or sombre? Is there a light source in the picture and are parts of the picture deliberately obscure or understated?

Being observant about just some of a painting's qualities can reveal significant tensions as well as correspondences that might exist between its form and content. For instance, the brushwork, tone, colour, perspective and positioning of figures might reinforce or subvert the subject matter.

Activity

Look at Bruegel's *Landscape with the Fall of Icarus* (Visual Sources, Plate IV).

- Does your knowledge of the Ovidian narrative affect your response to the painting?
- How would you describe its content if you were not familiar with the myth of Icarus?

Discussion

My first thought about the painting was the difficulty the viewer has in finding Icarus – even if we could stand in front of this large canvas the white legs disappearing into the water are hardly central. This is a busy but not a bustling landscape and I had a distinct sense of measured movement in the human activities Bruegel portrays. The influence of the bright Mediterranean dawn is very much in evidence in the scene but possibly the ploughman sports the richer hues of the Northern school of painting. I certainly felt drawn into the picture and invited not only to examine the world beyond this figure in the foreground but also to wonder how each of its parts or vignettes related to each other. The drowning boy is the only disturbance, a sudden and uncalculated event occurring in an otherwise (at first glance) tranquil setting.

Icarus is so close to the ship (this delicate craft is like almost everything in the picture, animate and inanimate alike, uncaring of the tragic death of the boy in the water) that if the viewer of the painting did not know the myth it would be reasonable to assume that Icarus was a man or sailor overboard. In that case the wonder of a boy falling from the sky has been transformed into a blip or a blot on the landscape.

In Peter Wagner's *Icons, Texts, Icontexts* there is yet another interpretation of Bruegel's almost mischievous depiction of Icarus. The somersaulting boy could be a swimmer happily disporting himself in contrast to the ploughman who is toiling away – the sort of sardonic comment Bruegel was fully capable of making about contrasts between the labouring peasantry and their wealthy 'betters' (Wagner, 1996, p. 276).

If you look Icarus up in your Penguin Dictionary you will find another version of the story, one in which Icarus followed his father from Athens by boat and was shipwrecked off Samos. There was also a tradition that Daedalus and Icarus sailed from Crete. So Bruegel may be following Ovid for the scene but suggesting a less miraculous method of escape for the exiles.

Ovid's tragic tale is very much marginalised (after all, the painting is called *Landscape* with *the Fall of Icarus*). Nor is there any sign of Daedalus. It was long thought that Daedalus had originally been included on the canvas, as it looked as if a high aerial figure had been subsequently painted over or painted out. The amazed spectators of the poem mind their own business in Bruegel.

So it is fair enough, I think, to ask what the point was of including Icarus at all. A simple answer would be that biblical and classical scenes were regarded as worthier subject matter for high art than a mere landscape. In theory the presence of Icarus elevates the genre Bruegel has chosen. In other paintings Bruegel marginalises momentous religious events in a similar way, focusing on environment and setting rather than the alleged subjects, such as the martyrdom of Christ or the journey of the Magi.

However, there is clearly a more complex agenda at work in all Bruegel's paintings and his relationship to Ovid's text is a subtle and subversive one. On closer inspection the partridge (Perdix) is in the picture (bottom right and on the branch above the angler preoccupied with his fishing) which demonstrates that Bruegel is consciously engaging with Ovid's narrative. The presence of the partridge reminds a viewer familiar with Ovid that Perdix was enjoying his moment of revenge. To complicate matters there is a counter-view that the partridge is not in fact looking towards Icarus but is as detached or unobservant as the other spectators.

In that case you may feel that the painting is pure parody and very far from the poignancy of Ovid's narrative. No one in it is noticeably concerned at the tragedy and the legs are positively comical. Bruegel certainly seems to be altering Ovid in his portrayal of the 'witnesses' to this incredible sight, men flying like gods. Only the shepherd is looking upwards and this is, in any case, a conventional way of portraying shepherds in art. As for the ploughman who clearly supplants Icarus as the painting's protagonist (and it is characteristic of Bruegel to promote everyday rural activities in this way), he bears out the German proverb that 'a farmer does not leave his plough for the sake of a dying man'. And if you look carefully, there is a skull halfway up the trunk of the fruit tree towards which the plough furrows run.

A further angle on the painting

Although all these human figures have been imported from Ovid, according to Christian Vöhringer, Bruegel has produced 'a pictorial cultural composition which comprises Flemish calendar motifs and there could well be a reference to the Athenian farmer Icarios and the spring constellation to which he belonged' (2007, p. 107). Bruegel has painted a young man at the plough who might be described as an incongruity in that he is 'festively' dressed. Vöhringer concludes that 'without the ploughman and his calendar significance the only mythological painting by Bruegel would be alien' (p. 110).

However, Bruegel may not be entirely distancing himself from the tragedy of Icarus. The painter produced several drawings and prints that relate to 'the artist' and he had a complicated relationship with sixteenth-century humanist traditions. He might have been drawn to Icarus as an overweening craftsman with little talent and so deliberately portrayed him in an undignified landing because this would be a just retribution of misplaced pride. But Bruegel did also produce a magnificent sketch of Icarus free falling in clear space which shows him as a muscular and heroic man rather than a weedy and callow youth.

For all these reasons the painter's reference to this particular myth in this particular painting must surely be motivated by more than an attempt to elevate his art in terms of the hierarchy of genres. My own quirky notion and an attempt to harmonise earnestness with jest and a dose of self irony, is that the white legs of Icarus could also function as an artist's signature from Bruegel, suggesting that however accomplished the painting is, any artist is liable to be raised and deflated in one fell swoop.

Auden and his work

Auden was one of a group of intellectual poets who hoped to prick the public conscience with their poetry. They promoted the cause of anti-fascism in the 1930s and, according to Stephen Spender, 'were the divided generation of Hamlets who found the world out of joint and failed to set it right' (1951, p. 202). Auden was poetically inspired by T.S. Eliot and he followed a similar technique of incorporating short poems into longer works. Eliot advised Auden not to apologise for rather recondite allusions, and Auden seemed to follow Eliot's style of composition as well as his sense of doom and resignation at a culturally impoverished and diminishing civilisation.

What to look for in the poem

The Auden poem you are about to read is composed in free verse and this can be a challenging form to analyse in purely 'technical' terms, but the following general guidelines should help you work out how the poet conveys his feelings on viewing the Bruegel painting.

A first relatively (or deceptively) straightforward question to ask is 'what is the poem about?'. Is it descriptive, reflective, a message of some sort or an outpouring of emotion? Is anyone specifically addressed? Does it work on more than one level of meaning and are we encouraged to read between its lines?

The technical skills employed by a poet are actually his or her artistry (and armoury) of expression. If there is no identifiable rhyme scheme or regular rhythm it could have quite a conversational feel. (This is also enhanced by the sense carrying over from line to line – called enjambment.) What type of language characterises the poem – archaic, specialised or colloquial – and are there any vivid, emotive or surprising choices of words?

If consonants are repeated (alliteration) or vowel sounds are repeated (assonance), and if there is only occasional rhyming or slant rhyme (similar sounding words but not quite a perfect match), what kind of effect does this have?

What about the figurative language of poetry and its impact on the reader? Does the poet use simile (an image in which one thing is likened to another; e.g. 'my love is like a red, red rose') or metaphor (where one thing is actually substituted for another; e.g. 'life is a walking shadow') to expand our visualisation and understanding of a scene or a situation?

Activity

Now read Auden's poem 'Musée des Beaux Arts' (Secondary Source I in Textual Sources 1).

- What kind of message do you feel Auden has received from Breugel's painting?

- Can you detect any vestiges of Ovid in Auden's literary response to *Landscape with the Fall of Icarus*?

Discussion

'About suffering they were never wrong,/The Old Masters,' is the arresting opening to Auden's poem. It is as if the reader has stumbled upon Auden's train of thought or that he has deliberately stopped us in our tracks with his musings. The poem masquerades as something conversational and so technically it is free verse (although there is a detectable, if lackadaisical, rhythm and rhyme scheme). The form of this poem – the continuous present of the verb in the first stanza (especially line 4); the flow of one line into the next (enjambment) – reflects and simultaneously reinforces the reverie-like state of the poet.

The second stanza constitutes a sonnet-like 'turn' (the *volta* which marks a change in direction, pace or tone) as the poet stands in front of *Landscape with the Fall of Icarus*. Auden's commentary on the Bruegel painting has been prefaced then by the common message he has found in a gallery of representations that refuse to foreground suffering and set even significant martyrdoms against scenes of 'life going on'.

The movement of the lines keep in step with Auden who seems to be circling around the paintings and then stopping in front of *Landscape with the Fall of Icarus*. Thinking back to Bruegel's technique of promoting surroundings over important historical subjects in other works, you might safely assume that Auden sees the painting as a centrepiece for human suffering that has no universal significance. Auden imports scenes from other Bruegel pictures to stress the general lack of interest from those engrossed in activities of the moment (lines 7–8 and 12–13).

The poet apparently accepts, even approves, the fact that Bruegel and the Flemish school of painters saw suffering as it really was, no great issue in the grand scheme of things. This is a bleak reaction on Auden's part but there might be some hint of comfort about the constancy of elemental things and the fact that the natural world keeps its core aspects unchanged whatever personal tragedies occur within it.

There is an alternative way of dealing with grief: the assumption that the natural world not only suspends all activity but that it might partake in the mourning. The notion that the natural world should grieve over individual bereavement is known as 'the pathetic fallacy' and Auden does seem to be up-ending this romantic view of a universe in tune with personal suffering. For Auden, Bruegel is the sane counterpoint to such a sentimental view of suffering; and yet Auden himself in his apparently heartfelt poem, commonly known as 'Stop All the Clocks' (Secondary Source II, which you can optionally read), demands that the world stop turning because of his personal loss, and that living creatures cease to carry on the daily round and routine.

In comparing Auden's two poems I was particularly struck by the insistence that in 'Stop All the Clocks' the dog should not enjoy his juicy bone (line 2) which is in stark contrast to line 12 of 'Musée des Beaux Arts', where dogs are depicted as going on with their 'doggy life'. In this respect Auden may be moving closer to the world of Ovid's *Metamorphoses* in which death or traumatic transformation of one creature can cause emotional and physical tremors across a landscape.

Further complications

It is worth noting that 'Stop All the Clocks' has received its iconic and sentimental status partly because of its appearance in the film *Four Weddings and a Funeral* (directed by Mike Newell, 1994). In the cinematic context it underscored a moving scene with the deceased's lover reciting the poem as a sincere lament (although those less taken with the film's relentless sequence of comic vignettes may have welcomed the moment as 'tragic relief'). But this is the beauty of 'reception', that it reinvents the original meaning and timbre of the text, as 'Stop All the Clocks' was most likely intended to be a pastiche of love in grief rather than a genuine outpouring of sorrow. The bereaved lover is demanding against all reason that time is suspended, and that cosmic and conventional activity ceases, but this is part of the helplessness and hopelessness of the human condition.

Although it would seem in 'Musée des Beaux Arts' that Auden identifies himself intimately with the painter's view of Icarus, there are moments when Ovid's *Metamorphoses* text reasserts itself. The forsaken cry (line 16) evokes the terror of Icarus and the helpless grief of Daedalus. Ovid's creation of a telescoped time frame, the joyous flight suddenly cut short as the boy plummets towards the water, is reflected in Auden's line.

Michael Riffaterre detects equivocation in Auden towards Bruegel's depiction of Icarus (1986, pp. 1–13). Riffaterre argues that Auden has reinstated Icarus in all his poignancy after buying into Bruegel's comical depiction of his deathly fall. Auden redirects our gaze to Icarus falling out of the sky which has no place in the narrative sequence of the painting. Auden identifies the body of the boy and gives him voice whereas the white legs in Bruegel completely anonymise him. Auden also suggests in this last stanza that the ship must have seen 'something amazing' and the reader is left with the abiding image of the boy falling out of the sky.

Riffaterre believes that 'Pointing to what is hidden in the landscape makes the description of the landscape a pretext to show what it is hiding' and he cites Auden's poetic principles: 'To me Art's subject is the human clay/And landscape but a background to a torso' (p. 9). In that case, there is a double bluff in Auden's focus on Icarus in the second stanza, in that he paradoxically restores him to centre stage. Riffaterre makes the interesting point that 'Auden's melodramatic focusing on a child's death eliminates the artist's symbolism' (p. 10). I think what Riffaterre is getting at is the choice Auden has made to restore the poignancy of Ovid's portrayal while praising the painter for downsizing the tragedy of an individual. The poet imagines 'the forsaken cry' and the very focus on the 'white legs' has already foregrounded them in our minds even if they are minimalised in the painting.

Riffaterre goes on to complicate the process further in that he believes Bruegel is making a statement about artistic failure; high-flying Icarus ends as a brushstroke in the painting but is still recognisable as an aspiring artist by the critical viewer. Icarus loses his status as a symbol in the Auden poem because he is simply, if unutterably sadly, the silly little boy who flew too close to the sun.

Both artist and poet, separated by centuries and huge cultural distances from Ovid, are still conducting a dialogue with their Roman source and simultaneously 'mything' Icarus for their own particular purposes. Roland Barthes argued that myth cannot really be grasped as an object, a concept or even an idea, but should be seen as a speech act, a message, a very specific sort of communication (1955, p. 93). In 2008 during an *In Our Time* programme (Melvyn Bragg, Radio 4) Professor Mary Beard echoed this approach to some extent by encouraging us to think of myth as a verb 'to myth' rather than as a noun, which perhaps gives this ever evolving aspect of human creative storytelling a misleading solidity and fixity. (You will learn more about the fluid and performative nature of myth in Block 4, when reading Graham Harvey's essay on myth and religion in Textual Sources 2.)

5.6   The labyrinthine nature of myth

Ovid could well be responsible for Icarus' afterlife as a figure representing human aspirations – his overreaching ends in a heroic failure which is nevertheless more frequently admired than condemned. Ovid does not portray Icarus in this way, however, and it is ironic that Icarus has become conflated with his highly skilled father (an artist by association) because in the traditional tale Daedalus' disappointment in his son's complete lack of talent was palpable and exacerbated his hostility towards his gifted nephew.

We cannot be sure of the sequence of events but it is possible that the reappearance of Icarus in *Metamorphoses* – which was being composed some years after the poet had already told the story in the *Ars Amatoria* (*The Art of Love*) – relates to the poet's personal circumstances. Ovid's banishment to Tomis on the Black Sea and his own predicament gave new meaning to Daedalus' desire for breaking his bonds and the boundaries of land and sea to fly home (though the emperor barred the ways).

In that case, and at a later date, the myth of Daedalus and Icarus might well have had a personal resonance for Ovid as the poet himself fell from grace through artistic exuberance. Ovid's celebrity status at Rome brought him into close proximity with 'heavenly bodies' (if one can describe the emperor Augustus and his family in that way). Ovid then plummeted from the position of great literary eminence (something akin to Rome's poet laureate) to the state of disgraced exile.

In the opening lines of Book 2 of *The Art of Love*, Ovid discusses how hard it is to pin down a winged love god (lovers have the dice loaded against them) and compares Cupid with Daedalus who made an escape on artificial wings. As an optional extra you can read this (on the face of it) very similar version of the Icarus story in Primary Source I (Textual Sources 1) (although note that the translation is by A.D. Melville and you may find his poetically structured narrative takes a little bit of unravelling). The metrical scheme of *The Art of Love* is different from the epic hexameter of *Metamorphoses* which is a more stately and fluid measure for matters of serious import. The elegiac couplet was used in lament and poetry of a more personal nature and it also suits a work purporting to teach as it lends itself to shorter statements – a discrete thought or sentiment for every two lines.

This earlier introduction of the Daedalus story into *The Art of Love* is somewhat eccentric and the motivation is, quite frankly, forced. This was a light-hearted work on strategies for seduction, which apparently contributed to the poet's exile although Ovid's banishment occurred ten years after its publication. *The Art of Love* was presented in mock didactic form and style; that is, as a teaching manual for the successful conduct of affairs with women regardless of their status and citizenship.

In yet another rather bizarre digression in *The Art of Love* Ovid uses Pasiphaë to illustrate how easy it is to arouse passion in a woman (optionally see Primary Source II in Textual Sources 1). In general, Ovid and those close contemporaries who also chose to concentrate on writing love poetry allude to divine and heroic figures in unlikely poetic places with the clear expectation that their readers would supply the story, and also engage with the most relevant aspect of the myth for the dramatic scenario. The poets used myths to tease out the mood swings of lovers, to mock themselves and their mistresses, to explore darker and more dangerous areas of passion and mutual manipulation in highly charged relationships. It has long been recognised that myths can function in this psychological, almost therapeutic way in all kinds of different societies and cultures.

In Block 1 you will be reading a further sample of Ovidian elegiac poetry: a letter of seduction penned by Phaedra to her stepson, justifying her forbidden passion. Ovid's epistles by mythical heroines constitute an unusual and intriguing poetic corpus in which long-suffering and maligned women are represented with a contemporary Roman air of sophistication.

5.7   Conclusion

I hope that this talk-through of three ways of narrating a myth and the rich interaction of its representations in very different cultural contexts centuries apart has given you some sense of the complexity of a myth's function and meaning. As many of us will have encountered Greek and Roman myths in our childhood, we may occasionally feel that the complex categorisations and the search for subtle meanings in familiar stories can constitute the death of innocence in the face of theory. However, there is no reason why we should not derive great pleasure from reading from the outset with a critical perspective; Ovid's narratives do not simply invite us, they compel us to do just that.

When you start your study of Block 1 you will find further and equally lively debates about our understanding of Greek myth but the questions become more specific and less overarching, bringing in fascinating features such as the relationship of myth to cults and rituals. This preliminary exercise with Ovid has, in part, prepared you for the role played by Athenian drama (which you will be studying next); their tragic playwrights could readily reconfigure narratives of myth in a medium designed to disturb and dislodge their audiences from the comfort zone of the familiar and expected.

References

Andrews, R. (2001) *Icarus*, London, Little, Brown.

Barthes, R. (1993) 'Myth today' in Sontag, S. (ed.) *A Barthes Reader*, London, Vintage.

Beard, M. (2008) 'The Greek myths', *In Our Time* (presented by Melvyn Bragg), BBC radio programme, 13 March.

Davidson, J. (2007) 'Icarus falling', *Afternoon Play*, BBC radio programme, 25 July.

Larkin, P. (1982) *Required Writing: Miscellaneous Pieces 1955–1982*, London, Faber.

March, J.R. (1998) *Cassell Dictionary of Classical Mythology*, London, Cassell.

Melville, A.D. (trans.) (1986) *Ovid: Metamorphoses*, Oxford, Oxford University Press.

Reid, J.D. (ed.) (1993) *Oxford Guide to Classical Mythology in the Arts, 1300–1990s*, vol. 1, New York and Oxford, Oxford University Press.

Riffaterre, M. (1986) 'Textuality: W.H. Auden's "Musée des Beaux Arts"' in Caws, M.A. (ed.) *Textual Analysis: Some Readers Reading*, New York, MLA.

Spender, S. (1951) *World within World*, London, Hamish Hamilton.

Vöhringer, C. (2007) *Masters of Netherlandish Art: Pieter Bruegel*, Königswinter, Tandem Verlag.

Wagner, P. (1996) *Icons, Texts, Icontexts: Essays on Ekphrasis and Intermediality*, Berlin and New York, Walter de Gruyter.

Optional reading

Davisson, M.H.T. (1997) 'The observers of Daedalus and Icarus in Ovid', *Classical World*, vol. 90, no. 2/3, pp. 263–78.

Pavlock, B. (1998) 'Daedalus in the labyrinth of Ovid's *Metamorphoses*', *Classical World*, vol. 92, no. 2, pp. 140–57.

A330 team

Academic team

Professor Chris Emlyn-Jones, A330 chair and author
Dr Val Hope, A330 chair and author
Dr Felix Budelmann, author (Magdalen College, Oxford)
Dr Jessica Hughes, author
Dr Janet Huskinson, author
Dr Paula James, author

External assessor

Dr Susan Deacy (Roehampton University, London)

Tutor assessor

Martin Thorpe

Production team

Charlotte Adams, editor
John Berriman, website administrator
Gail Block, consultant sound and vision producer (Clear Focus Productions)
Carole Brown, sound and vision assistant
Eleanor Clark, visual resources project officer
Kate Clements, proofreader
Andrew Coleman, copy-editor
Lene Connolly, print buyer
Fabienne Evans, curriculum manager
Lizzy Gray, sound and vision producer
Peter Heatherington, graphic designer
Paul Hillery, graphic designer
Beate Lie, curriculum manager
Andrew McDermott, media assistant
Mark Ockenden, curriculum manager
Sheila Page, media project manager
Nikki Smith, assistant print buyer
Jeremy Taylor, interactive media developer
Andrew Whitehead, graphic artist
Nicky Woolgar, curriculum assistant